By Laura Williams
Translated By Wang Ling

睡觉

[shuìjiào] – to sleep

洗澡

[xǐzǎo] – to take a bath

爬行

[páxíng] – to crawl

玩

[wán] – to play

坐下

[zuò xià] - to sit

哭泣

[kū qì] – to cry

站起来

[zhàn qǐ lái] - to stand

鼓掌

[gǔ zhǎng] - to clap

阅读

[yuèdú] – to read

吃东西

[chī dōng xī] – to eat

喝东西

[hēdōng xī] – to drink

大笑

[dàxiào] – to laugh

拥抱

[yōng bào] – to hug

步行

[bùxíng] – to walk

跑

[pǎo] – to run

亲吻

[qīnwěn] - to kiss

跳

[tiào] – to jump

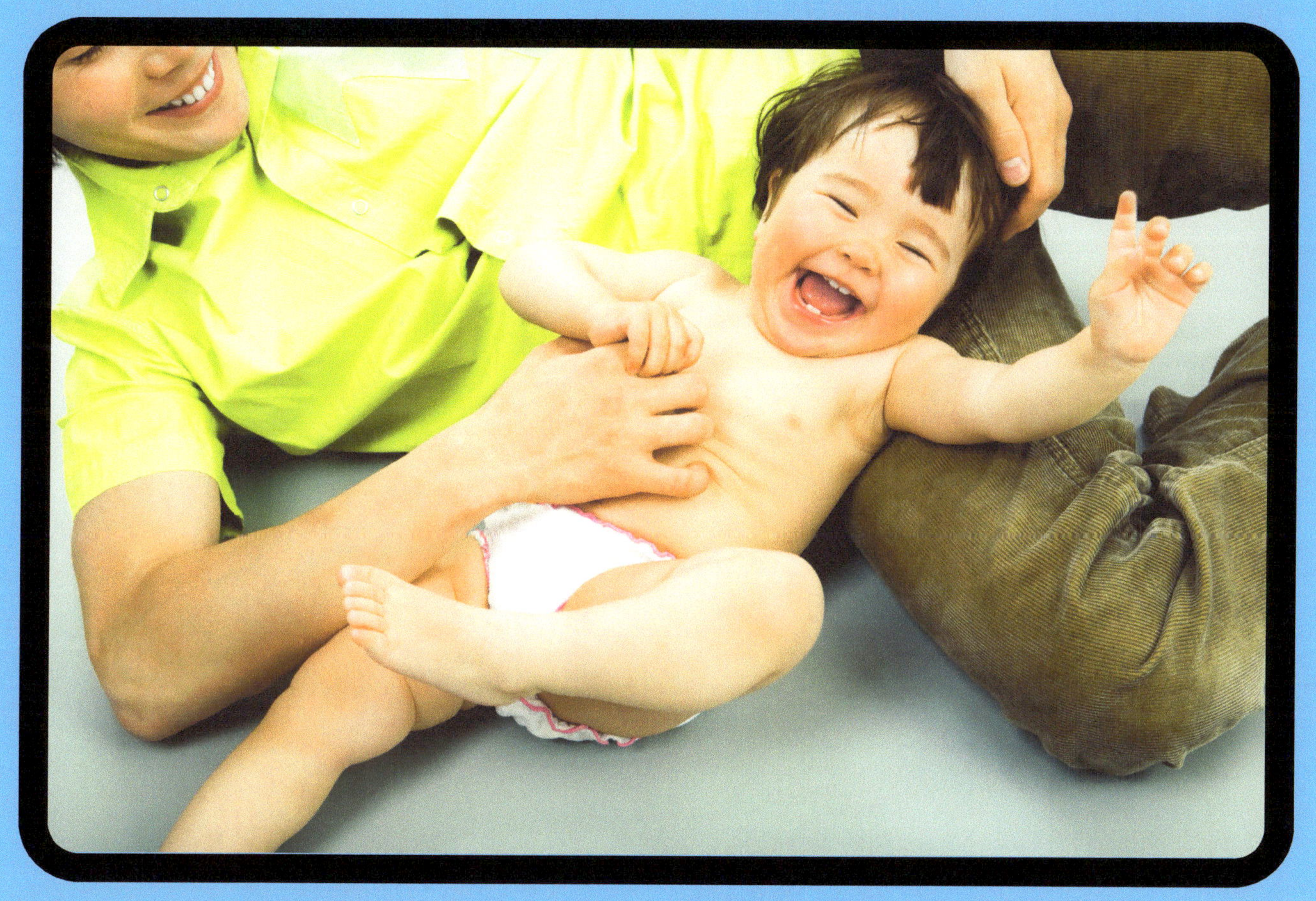

搔痒

[sāo yǎng] – to tickle

跳舞

[tiào wǔ] – to dance

做饭

[zuò fàn] – to cook

跪下

[guì xià] – to kneel

推

[tuī] – to push

拉

[lā] – to pull

写

[xiě] – to write

唱歌

[chàng gē] – to sing

In the same collection

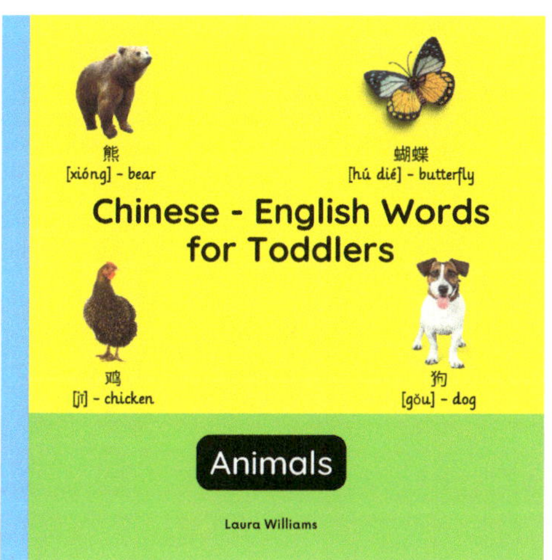

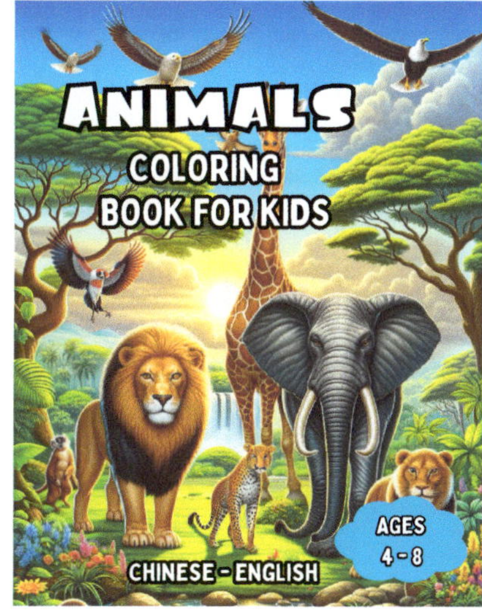

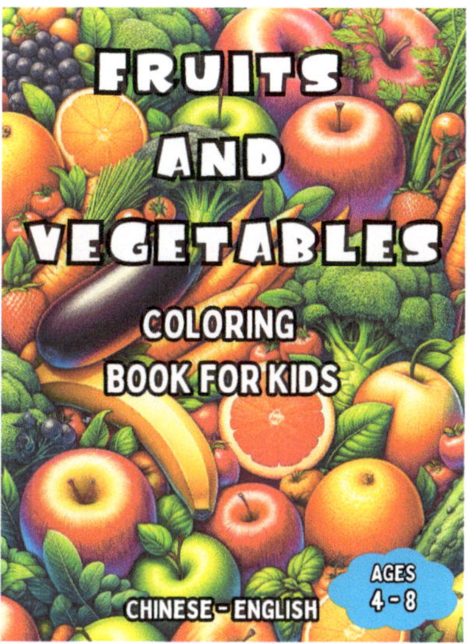